for me.
may I always be my
own first choice.

THE ASTRONAUT AND THE ROSE-COLORED HELMET

RACHAEL LORD

Nymeria Publishing LLC

First published in the United States of America by Nymeria

Publishing LLC, 2025

Nymeria Publishing

PO Box 350747

Jacksonville, Fl 32235

Visit our website at www.nymeriapublishing.com

Print ISBN 9781969098000

Ebook ISBN 9781969098017

1st Edition

Printed in U.S.A

the astronaut and the rose-colored helmet

the astronaut
stands outside the earth
bound by protective layers
of self-soothing words.

their rose-colored helmet
casts the world in loving shades.
their smile can be seen
from every galaxy.

the astronaut
places both hands
on either side of her helmet
lifts and removes.

when the dust settles
when at last her vision is clear

the astronaut
weeps.

I

december 31, 2022

this year,
my only hope
is to exist
in the notion that everything
will be okay

and that
i will survive this.

the stars look different

even though
there is magic
to be found

everywhere

there is danger
to be found
in every little
glimmer—

the stars look
different
from up here.

alternative alignment

i wonder if
everything
would be
different
had the stars aligned
themselves
another way
that night.

but to face
that reality
is to always wonder
what if

and to always
ponder
the alternative
alignment.

space / time

i thought i could explore
space and time

by wearing a helmet
with a rosy sheen.

i thought i could love
the same way, too

but traveling through space
& following my heart

required more than my eyes alone
could see.

the villain of my own story

i am a good person
a decent person
an *okay* person

but i don't know how to be
everything i want
without being
perceived as the
villain.

haunting I

every time i remember
your voice,
the sound sends
shockwaves
down my
spine.

The syllables continue
to haunt me

even now.

coping slowly

how do i cope knowing
that i won't grow old
with you

how i do breathe feeling
like i've failed
with you

how the *fuck*
do i move on
without you

i loved everything about you.

and i wish,
god,
how i wish,
that was
enough.

asteroid

part of me wonders
why i ever came back to Earth
if only to have my heart
wrecked by an
asteroid.

for the weak

marriage and love
are not for the weak.

if i could tell my younger
self that very phrase,
perhaps she wouldn't have been
weakened
by fairytales and cosmos.

going to a wedding when you're separated

celebrating the love
of close friends—
they smile and say,
"we can't wait to be like you."

we smile, too,
so they don't see
that there isn't always

happily ever after.

going to a wedding when you're separated II

that bright, young
twenty-two year old
clinging on to joy
was someone i knew
fondly.

what i'd give
to go back to that day
when the world had yet to
sink its teeth into my skin

and i was everything
i dreamed of being
with a whole life
to set me free.

bravery

i am not brave
for falling in love

i am not braver
for standing up for myself

i am not weaker
for staying

i am not stronger
for leaving

blindsided

the sun rises
without warning

and i am
blinded.

let me tear down
the stars

one by one
in an effort
to give you space.

it was supposed to be you

rocking chairs and
coffee mugs,
babies on the porch, a
white picket fence
in the suburbs.

who i am

i have no idea
who i am without you
and that scares me
in more ways than
i could ever
explain.

overgiver, underloved

i wish i could've been everything
you needed.

i'm sorry
i couldn't give you more
of myself
but there was simply
nothing
left.

mom was right

i was too young
to know better
and to know
myself.

kitchen table heart

i hate that i had to
bare my heart
on the kitchen table
like it wasn't beaten, bloody,
mangled and *gray*

as if hurting you
hurt me any less.

in another life

we would lay on a bed
of roses,
hands entwined
for eternity.

and you would tell me
how much you loved
the way the sunlight
framed my face in just
the right way

and we would never
wonder where the sunlight
came from
in the first place.

a galaxy i'll never know

i'll never see the vastness
of the
universe

and that will
have to be
okay.

killed you, darling

i killed the poems
i wrote about

you

didn't deserve my body
my heart
and certainly not
my fucking
art.

i swore i'd never end up
like my parents.

promised myself that i'd
stick it out,
beat the statistics.

but now i'm just
their spitting image.

lightyears away

if you and i
are made of the same
particles of stardust, then
why are we on opposite sides
of the sky?

so what

i'm just supposed to pretend
you never existed?

no caller id

we said our vows
before god
but now i don't recognize
your voice.

two pretenders

see, we were two pretenders
fooling the world
(and ourselves)

but damnit
we tried,
gave it everything
we had.

my first night alone

was like starting over
from the beginning of time,
before i knew everything or
anything at all.

i sat on the couch
our couch, and
pondered each decision that led
me to this moment.

my first night alone,
i kissed my old life goodbye.
i slept alone
with only the fan
to sing me to sleep.

getting ready for my divorce hearing

is like putting on clothes
for my own
funeral. i slip on a black,
floral dress and old shoes that are
comfortable but not too nice. i don't
wear makeup for fear that even that
would be ruined.

the breakable vows

i wrote
the most beautiful vows
i cried
on our wedding day

i cried
when you left
but like you,
i did not look back.

phantom ring

absentmindedly,
i rub the space
on my left ring finger
where a diamond once sat.

i do this without realizing
how long i went
with the safety of this
ritual.

i do this without knowing
the last time i felt such
comfort.

i do this with the knowledge
that there once was
gold and now there is
only
skin.

II

initiation into the young ex wives club

the funny thing
about being
a twenty-six year old divorcee
is that i have so much love
ahead of me,
to give
and to wish for

but an entire
girlhood
to mourn.

love for the liar

we tell ourselves
that love exists
in an effort to make us believe
the world isn't shit.

i tell myself because
if it *is* real
then i don't have to stop
telling stories of it.

it will all work out.

let me repeat that
it will work out.

somehow
someway.

rose-colored love

i thought i knew
what my heart
needed / desired

but the hues created
blind spots.

truth & a lie

i had forgotten
what it was like to fall
in love,
to teeter between holding
your heart
as a truth,
a lie,

or a combination
of both.

sky full of stars

there are more stars
than one could ever need,
yet i find myself
looking at one

you
searching for you
wishing for you

even still
even so.

greek tragedy

i have read our story
hundreds of times
hoping that the ending
might be different.

yet the words never change,
the characters never find their way
back to each other.

but i'll keep reading
hoping that there's something i missed
between the lines.

but i'll keep reading
hoping that i misread blurry
words, wet with tears.

maybe this time
the story might have a
happier ending.

in another life II

our house would be filled
with love, laughter, and
legacy.

we would smile.
you would hold me close,
and say,

look what we made.

starry eyed lover

you have stolen the stars
and placed them where my eyes
should be.

you have stolen my breath
and replaced it with
stardust.

you have stolen my heart
and made a constellation
of the broken pieces.

all i can give

is home and
love, comfort
and laughter,
little ones,
and a house full of dogs.

but if that isn't
what you want
then why do we keep
bothering?

all you could give

is the life i dream of
but i'm not sure
i could do the same
for you

despite my best
efforts to convince
you otherwise.

you are saturn

and i am earth's moon, so
desperate to be pulled
into your orbit.

long distance

you'll follow your dreams
and i'll follow mine
because the stars align for us

i think we'll be
just fine

right?

THE ASTRONAUT AND THE ROSE-COLORED HELMET

houston,
we have a problem
indeed.

see, i want to come back
to earth, but i am
afraid.

i am afraid because nobody
listens— nobody listens and
nobody has taught
me how to cope with pain
like this.

nobody ever taught me
how to grieve
someone still
alive.

nobody told me that there is more
to being alive than
staying alive.

houston...
are you still there?

my map of stars

is you. i trace each
constellation with my fingertip,
plot each voyage,
place each memory,
wonder how i got so lucky
to chart and know the stars
like i do.

gravitational attraction

our eyes lock
and my heart pulls slowly
then all at once,
like i was meant to be wrapped
in your gravity.

our hands touch
and i forget that there are
forces who do not
wish us to feel
this way,
that we must resist
the kinetic energy.

but
i cannot escape
the velocity
of you.

divinity

perhaps
we were always meant
to meet this way

perhaps
the fates divined it
said,
here's something
worth fighting for.

lessons in space travel

time
does not stop
for the weary traveler.

time
does not grant freedom
to make things happen
quickly, or at all.

time
is the enemy
of the space traveler.

time
is abundance and
scarcity

and longing
for something your heart
must be patient for.

wishing

i only wish
to be wanted
the way i want
you.

to be loved forever
the way i might always
love you.

**i don't know
what the future holds**

but i can say
with utmost certainty
that i never expected you.

i never expected
to meet you or know
you or love
you

if that counts
for anything.

frequency

the astronaut waits for the call
that will bring them back to earth.

they spend minutes upon
hours, upon
days in agony,
wondering if this will be the moment
they will hear the voice
that pulls them back from their exploration.

the astronaut waits for the call.
she conducts an experiment to keep busy.
she sleeps upright in the shuttle for as long as it takes.

waiting
waiting
waiting

burning moonlight

from dusk until dawn
i wait, a silent sleeper
in a dream that revolves
around you.

the moon is a welcome friend,
reminding me that one more day
has passed. i am one day closer
to feeling human again.

space explorers

i want to travel
to every galaxy,
every star,
every solar system with you

like two astronauts
lost in space
with nothing but time.

in another life III

i wouldn't have to wonder
what it would be like to be
yours.

i could be
with you completely and
the world would not
cast a sideways glance
or offer a word
of warning.

and i hate that i can't
have you
in every way,
as soon as possible,

right now.

in another life IV

i could sit here
and say:
in another life
it would be you
and me.

but when i look
at you,
i wonder why
another life
has to be anything
but this one.

when i stop loving you

know that i'll take
back the pieces of my heart
slowly. perhaps, i'll leave one
with you for safe keeping

just in case you change
your mind.

lack of oxygen

i don't want to suffocate you,
but my own lungs are crushed
under this weight of uncertainty.

i don't want to suffocate you.
i just want to breathe.

frequency II

i replay every conversation
every word and moment
that offered me the life i dreamed of

knowing now that i must let
them go, and

pretend they never existed,
pretend i never heard them
at all.

in another life V

i hope to be in a reality
where our souls
don't reach for each other
across stars and planets

where our hearts
aren't bonded
through all of space
and time.

passerby

i tell myself
that what is meant for me
will not pass me by

but the words feel like an
empty threat,
a sound that doesn't reach
my ears.

space / time II

if space is what you need
to find what you're looking for

to exhaust all efforts
and come back to yourself,

then i'll set you free
in the hope that you'll find
your way home

all in good time.

you taught me

bad habits.

i. halfway sleeping so i could
hear my phone ring in the dead of night

ii. second guessing if today would be the day
you'd decide not to want me

iii. little words i repeated over and over again,
like a mantra, filled with meaning— did you mean them, too?

iv. imagining a future with you

i won't beg you to stay.

i don't have it in me
to fight for someone
who would let me go
like it was easy,
like i wasn't what you wanted,
the one you waited your
entire life for.

i guess
this life wasn't the one
you were talking about.

lessons in space travel II

on every shooting star,
asteroid, airplane,
space shuttle
& cosmic ray

i am wishing
that you won't be just
another lesson learned

please don't be
another lesson

please stay

III

the hardest lessons

are the ones we didn't ask to
learn,
the ones we thought
we'd never have to.

fuck the planes,
the cosmic rays,
the shooting stars,
and asteroids.

and all the stars

in the sky
could not light up
the darkness
that your absence
has left
in my bones.

i had that funny feeling

and i knew,
in the deepest part of my soul
that it was never meant to be you & i.

i knew it would come to an end,
yet i still hoped
for a different outcome.

i knew you would break my heart,
yet i prayed
i was wrong.

i hate you

for leaving me like this:
broken, anxious, terrified.

i hate you for leaving me
so damaged and bruised and sour
and fucking hellbent
on survival.

i hate you for not calling me
when i needed you.

i hate you for calling me
only when you needed me.

i hate you for existing
just out of reach. in a facebook status
or in the back of someone else's photo.

i hate you for existing
at all.

and i hate that once i was so glad
that you did.

**i will live the rest of my life
without you.**

as if i did not watch you sleep every night for years,
as if i did not see the rest of my life by your side.

i will live the rest of my life without you
because the rest of my life and the rest of yours
did not line up on the atlas
of our two existences.

i will live the rest of my life without you,
pretending that it's better to have loved and lost
than never to have loved—
from strangers, to friends, to lovers
and back. so the story goes:

here's to new beginnings
and living my life
without you.

lessons in space travel III

one person's voyage to the moon
is another's painstaking
view, as they watch someone they once loved
make meaning of the sky

without them.

shatter / ing

the astronaut never
could have imagined
that the rose colored
glass surrounding their life
was anything but real.

when it shattered around them
there was nothing left
but blood

and clarity.

fun / ny

can someone tell me
the punchline to this joke
of life?

it isn't so funny
anymore.

marathons & moonbeams

i'm tripping over
stars
in a race back to
you.

silent sky

i begged the universe
for a sign,
a message that i'd be okay.

i screamed for healing
i wished for hope
i cried out for love

and each time,
i was met
with silence.

they call her space girl

because she is a galaxy of stars
on a clear night.

an asteroid,
the milky way,
and the moon combined.

she is night and day,
a summertime
solstice
baby.

she is a goddamn
lunar eclipse
and then some.

clear skies

the stars
shine brighter
on a clear night

love does,
too.

passerby II

in every person that passes
on the sidewalk, the highway,
the grocery store, train station—
i am reminded that life
is bigger than you, it is bigger
than me.

it is bigger than those
who come into your life
if only to pass you by
and pretend their purpose
was to do only that.

at times like this

i wonder if i ever really knew
how important i was
at the beginning.

if you asked

i'd collect each star,
hold them tight until you were ready
to claim them.

if you asked
i'd make moonbeams
out of uncertainty,
craft a constellation
of this beautiful mess.

if you asked
i would be yours
until the stars decided
to give up their light,
until they no longer burned
for you and me.

but lucky for me

i did not have to put myself
through such torment.

because,
you see,
the stars never burned for us
at all.

and for that,
i am so grateful.

all my ghosts

are stargazers
who lost themselves
to the sky.

mad woman

i am a woman
who exists out of spite
for those who tried to break
me, for those who succeeded
but left so i could pick up the pieces,
rearrange my shattered heart
into seven letters:

fuck you.

it was supposed to be you II

how do i move on
knowing that i was
wrong?

it was supposed to be you III

i may live a life
of aching regret
wondering who we'd be
had it been

right person, right time.

hellfire & starlight

honestly
i don't feel much
at all—
i hold on to grudges
and i don't let them

go,
find someone
who will hold your hand
in the dark

who will exist as starlight
and not as
hellfire.

yeah, i'm happy

that my heart is healing
and breaking in the same
beat, that my joy, sadness, and
aching work in tandem
to create beautiful
art

like this.

that my nights are filled
with laughter and coconut rum,
my words clinging with honesty,
my heart laying flat on my sleeve.

yeah, i'm happy.
why wouldn't i be?

playground space shuttle, circa 2002

our legs dangle and touch the grass. we grin from
ear to ear, like long lost friends.
from here, i count each freckle and all her
missing teeth. i soak in her smile
like patient sunshine, not too bright, nor too scalding. i hold
her small, unscarred hand. the patter of her steady heart
thrums slowly through her veins—
we jump —
suspended midair,
like two flightless birds.

are we going to be okay?
the little girl asks,
when we have landed once again.

i think so,
i reply.

how do you know?

i shake my head.
i don't know,
i say, and it's true.

i don't know how to tell her
that we'll be okay
because we have to.

haunting II

i am your ghost
or rather your shadow

but it's true:
i'm haunting myself
instead of you.

lessons in space travel IV

sometimes the best views
are the ones you get to witness
by yourself.

i saw Orion last night —
it was just him and me
and nothing else
mattered.

cosmic void

i refuse to write
another word
about you

because you have taken
more than your fair share
of my breath
my heart
my time
my joy
my words

and i wish you nothing
but silence.

THE ASTRONAUT AND THE ROSE-COLORED HELMET

a letter to myself on valentine's day

sweet girl,
you are stronger and braver than you think.
your heart is not empty or void of love—
it is only broken.
that does not mean that you will not find your way
or rearrange the pieces
to make a new masterpiece.

on a day like today
you are reminded that
you have more capacity for love
than you ever thought possible.

when you hold yourself tight,
drink your favorite coffee,
buy yourself two books and a bouquet of flowers,
and fall in love with the woman you
have become.

but it won't be easy.
you will be reminded, too,
of your shortcomings, your mistakes,
and the aching in your chest.

give yourself grace.
time to breathe.
another cup of coffee.

because you are
worthy of *that*
great love.

dancing in the moonlight

if i can love myself
the way i was always meant
to be loved

perhaps i'll always feel
good enough.

perhaps i'll always feel
worthy of dancing in the
moonlight.

maybe

i'm not meant
for love.

maybe
i was always meant
for myself.

on the pursuit
of love and destiny

i feel
that i will break my own heart
over and over again
in this journey.

i think
that in order to find
what i need, i'd shatter this old heart
until i can finally repair it
myself.

men on the moon

if we put men on the moon,
then how have we not found a cure
for heartbreak?

they foolishly say
that the cure is time,
but there isn't enough of it.
there never is.

how many trips to the moon
will it take until i'm whole
again?

me on the moon

i'll voyage
with only the stars to guide
me

with the whole world
just out of reach

all the better
to watch it turn
slowly

in the hope
that i can make sense
of why it turns
at all.

the sky is a storm

love
came to me in a moment
of fury and weakness—
blindsided, i was blinded
by you.

and in all my rage,
i found something much better
than anything you could offer me.

the storm was untapped strength,
and now she rages on.

to catch a fallen star

i fall from the
blue black sky

and nobody is
there to catch me.

i scream into the
darkest of nights

and nobody is
there to hear me.

i stumble into the
river below

and nobody is
there to save me.

i float through the
crushing expanse of the universe

and nobody is
there to guide me back.

i let my heart lead into the
darkest, blue black

and nobody is
there to catch me.

i don't know what the future holds II

in fact,
i thought i would be well
on my way to a simple life,
a comfortable silence
that left me no other choice

and not tangled
in a mess
of my own doing.

i am waltzing to the sound of a heart breaking

but the noise comes from somewhere
i can't quite hear,
a vibration of sorts
that is just out of reach

one, two, three
one, two, three

a lump forms in my throat,
my arms tremble and fall

i am waltzing to the sound
of *my own* heart
breaking.

a letter to her on her wedding day

sweetheart,
you look like a goddamn princess, and i mean that.
in every sense of the word. you grew up on fairytales
and happily ever afters
and princes
and shining armor
and true love's kiss.
and look at you now.
(how do I tell her?)

that dress was something you picked out three years
before you even got engaged.
it seemed like a dream. too expensive, but you found
a sample sale. the dress of your dreams.
dreams. it's all a dream.
that sounds like fate, right?
like the stars were always meant to align?
you fought for this.
you fought to be here, to be here with him.
and he is looking at you like he's never seen another star.
(how do I tell her that it will fade?)

sweetheart,
i beg you to enjoy this day.
and you will. because it's the start
of a journey you didn't expect.
the way you're looking at the stars tonight
is not the same way you'll look at them years later.
(life has a funny way of dimming starlight, baby.)

nobody
goes in to their wedding day

expecting to get a divorce.
nobody
expects to choose themselves instead.
(some don't have the courage.)

but you will and do, baby.
you will choose yourself.
and you will be okay.
enjoy these next four years,
sweetheart.
i wish i could make them different.
i wish i could offer a better outcome.

but truth is,
i'm still finding that outcome
for myself.

falling into darkness

means losing your sense
of time
and hoping that a beam of light
exists somewhere beyond
the deep black skies.

it means knowing
in the pockets of your heart
that the light will shine
again.

i thought i had tasted heartbreak.

i thought i knew what it felt like
to be irrevocably torn to pieces
and left to bleed.

i thought i knew heartbreak before,
but i was wrong.

i didn't know heartbreak then,
but i know it
now.

exhaustion

i'm tired of strength. i'm tired of being
resilient. i'm tired of loving too much for too
long. i'm tired of hoping, of waiting, of wanting.
i'm tired of the lessons learned. i'm tired of existing
with a broken heart. i'm tired of still wearing it
on my sleeve anyway. i'm tired of healing. i'm tired
of/from the grieving. i'm tired of aching for you.
i'm tired of wondering if you think about me. i'm tired
of wishing you loved me the way i loved you. i'm tired
i'm tired i'm so so fucking tired.

normal again

i wish i could safely
come back home
without feeling like i failed
to find the stars.

constellations

are where everything connects,
makes sense—

i can't believe
i spent so long looking
at the wrong one.

there are blindspots

where my telescope
cannot reach

where the astronaut floats
without gravity
and cannot see

the danger that
lies ahead.

THE ASTRONAUT AND THE ROSE-COLORED HELMET

i will never be
an astronaut

but now i see the world
the galaxies
the stars
the sun
the moon
for what they are

imperfect,
by chance

just like me.

lessons in space travel V

i will not be anyone's second choice.
i will not be lost to a love that doesn't deserve me.
i will not be stranded by my own pain.
i will not be blinded so that others can see.

earth goddess in an astronaut suit

for the first time
in my life,
i cherish the woman
looking back at me.

she is beautiful,
strong,
cosmic and bold.

she has battled the stars
and teetered
on moon beams.
asteroids and black holes
are simply no match for her.

she is an earth goddess
in an astronaut suit
meant to discover
all there is
to life, and love,
and cosmic existence.

i don't know what the future holds III

i'm terrified
of what lies ahead—
the darkness and star systems
yet to explore.

all that which ten years
could not have prepared me
to endure
or feel
or know that i'm capable of
on my own.

but i'll be damned
if i'm not a little curious
as to what this journey
looks like.

is it possible to hold a star
or fall asleep on a moonbeam?

is it possible to find a human hand
worthy of keeping my tired heart?

as i turn to the next constellation
i hope the words come easy
and well.
i hope I find my heart in
the next galaxy.

The Astronaut and the Rose Colored Helmet **PLAYLIST:**

1. Just Married- Kelsea Ballerini
2. tolerate it- Taylor Swift
3. Complex- Katie Gregson-Macleod
4. I miss you, I'm sorry- Gracie Abrams
5. loml- Taylor Swift
6. real love, to roommates (demo)- everything we do
7. Vortex- Lizzy McAlpine
8. Men on the Moon- Chelsea Cutler
9. About You- The 1975
10. we can't be friends (wait for your love)- Ariana Grande
11. the grudge- Olivia Rodrigo
12. Waiting Room- Phoebe Bridgers
13. Mountain With A View- Kelsea Ballerini
14. Down Bad- Taylor Swift
15. letters to an old poet- boygenius

ACKNOWLEDGMENTS

To Kennedy and Sarah, thank you for believing in my work. I am truly so grateful for your friendship, your support, and everything that you've done for me over these last several years. Working with you both and being a part of the Nymeria family is nothing short of a dream come true.

To Mom, thank you for showing me the courage to choose myself. Thank you for being a beacon in a very dark time and for teaching me that I can do anything. You continue to lead the way for me.

To James, I love you with my whole heart. Thank you for showing me that love exists after heartbreak.

To you, thank you for reading these words. Whether you see yourself as the astronaut or not, I hope you always, always, always choose yourself.

About the Author

Rachael Lord (she/her) is a writer and professional actress from Fort Myers, Florida. She has a BFA in Musical Theatre from Florida Southern College and an MFA in Creative Writing from Lindenwood University. Rachael's published works include: *Fragile Hearts Club* (Nymeria Publishing, 2021) and *The Meaning of Stars* (Nymeria Publishing, 2023). When she's not writing, Rachael enjoys spending time with her two dogs, playing Stardew Valley, and watching reality television.

instagram.com/therachael_lord

ALSO BY RACHAEL LORD

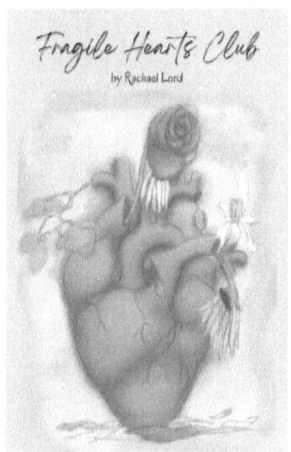